# PAN-WORSHIP

## AND OTHER POEMS

BY

ELEANOR FARJEON

LONDON

ELKIN MATHEWS, VIGO STREET, W.

1908

# CONTENTS

# PAN-WORSHIP

In Arcady there lies a crystal spring
Ring'd all about with green melodious reeds
Swaying seal'd music up and down the wind.
Here on its time-defacèd pedestal
The image of a half-forgotten God
Crumbles to its complete oblivion.
The faithful and invariable earth
Tilts at the shrine her sacrificial cup,
Spilling libations from the brim that runs
The golden nectar of her daffodils
And rivulets of summer-breathing flow'rs.
O evanescent temples built of man
To deities he honoured and dethroned!
Earth shoots a trail of her eternal vine
To crown the head that men have ceased to honour.
Beneath the coronal of leaf and lichen
The mocking smile upon the lips derides
Pan's lost dominion; but the pointed ears
Are keen and prick'd with old remember'd sounds.
All my breast aches with longing for the past!
Thou God of stone, I have a craving in me
For knowledge of thee as thou wert in old
Enchanted twilights in Arcadia.

9

Arcadia ! it is the very music
Of the first spring-tide rippling its first wave
Over the naked, laughing baby world   .   .   .
Come again, thou sparkling spring-tide, come again,
Rush in and flood this autumn from my soul !
These waters welling at a dead God's shrine,
These happy waters bubbling limpid kisses,
Even with such bright and eager lips made wet
The hem of the earth's garment in the days
When earth was youthful and the Gods of Greece
In starry constellation crowned Olympus.
What drifting mists have veil'd the Olympian fires ?
What of the Gods of Greece ? and what of Greece ?
O virgin Greece, standing with naked feet
In the morning dews of the world against the light
Of an infant dawn ! old Greece, ever-young Greece,
The pagan in my blood, the instinct in me
That yearns back, back to nature-worship, cries
Aloud to thee ! I would stoop to kiss those feet,
Sweet white wet feet washed with the earth's first dews
And leaning ear to grass I would re-catch
Echoes of footsteps sounding down dim ages
For ever the music once they made on thee :
The flaming step of the young Apollo when,
With limbs like light and golden locks toss'd back
On a smooth ivory shoulder, he avenged
His mother's wrongs on Python : the dreaming step

Of Hylas in the woods of Mysia
Leading to sleep beneath sweet sylvan waters :
The laughing step of untrammell'd Atalanta
Spurning the ground before her golden capture :
Child-Proserpina stepping like a flower,
And the singing step of Syrinx fleeing—what ?
If thou couldst speak, neglected, sneering stone,
Thou wouldst know how to answer me.   Wilt thou
Not speak ?   .   .   .   How still it is !   .   .   .   The noise
　　of the world
Is shut about  with silence !   .   .   .   If I kneel,
Bend and adore, make sacrifice to thee,
If to thy long-deserted fane I  bring
Tribute of milk and honey—then if I snap
That loveliest pipe of all at the spring's margin
And let the song of Syrinx from its hollow,
Nay, even the nymph's sweet self—O Pan, old Pan,
Shall I not see thee stirring in the stone,
Crack thy confinement, leap forth—*be* again ?
I can believe it, master of bright streams,
Lord of green woodlands, king of sun-spread plains
And star-splashed hills and valleys drenched in moonlight !
And I shall see again a dance of Dryads
And airy shapes of Oreads circling free
To shy sweet pipings of fantastic fauns
And lustier-breathing satyrs   .   .   .   God of Nature,
Thrice hailing thee by name with boisterous lungs

I will thrill thee back from the dead ages, thus:
*Pan! Pan! O Pan! bring back thy reign again*
*Upon the earth!* . . .

               Numb pointed ears, ye hear
Only the wash and whisper of far waters,
The pale green waters of thin distant Springs
Under the pale green light of distant moons
Washing upon the shores of the old, old world
With a foam of flowers, a foam of whispering flowers .

# VAGRANT SONGS

## I

But yesterday the winds of March
Bent back the barren branches of the larch   .
          But O ! to-day
The bareness from the earth is swept away.


Deep through my swelling breast I hear
The wild call of the gipsy time o' year—
          O, Vagrant Spring,
Brother o' mine, I'm for the gipsying !


The greening earth I stand upon
Tingles my feet : Brother, we must begone !
          Younger and younger,
All my heart cries aloud with Wander-Hunger

## II

Of troubles know I none,
Of pleasures know I many—
I rove beneath the sun
Without a single penny.

A king might envy long
The fare my board adorning—
Upon a throstle's song
I broke my fast this morning;

My lunch, a girl's quick smile,
As I'm a living sinner;
She walked with me a mile  .
I kissed her for my dinner.

Of troubles know I none,
Of pleasures know I many—
I fare beneath the sun
Without a single penny!

## III

O, how she laughs with me,
Eats with me, quaffs with me,
Smiles to me, sighs to me,
Questions, replies to me,
Answers my every mood,
Finds good what I find good,
    Earth, the green Mother!

Where shall man live and die
Having my treasury
Which never gold could buy—
Water and air and sky
And Earth's great sympathy—
Save he do live as I?
　　Join with me, Brother!

If you be sickening
Here's for your quickening!
Here at the heart of it
You shall be part of it,
And the good smell of rain
Shall make you whole again—
　　Join with me, Brother!
Here the life-sap runs green,
Here the life-ways are clean,
Here just one bird that sings
Re-starts your sluggish springs,
Here under moon and sun
You, I and She are one,
　　Earth, the green Mother!

## IV

I lay me on the ground
              Under the dark,
And Heaven's purple arc
Drew its deep curtains round
My weary head and shut away the sound.

The golden star-lights crept
              Over the hill  .  .  .
I lay so very still
I heard them as they stepped  .  .  .
"Sleep!" breathed the Earth.    Upon her breast
    I slept.

## V

I'll stay one night beneath your roof,
And longer I will stay for no man,
And as for love, I'm loving-proof—
    Turn by your eyes, White Woman.

The Wander-fever's in my blood,
I have no time for simple loving—
The hot Earth is in roving mood,
    And I too must be roving.

*If* I should love you  .  .  .  soon, ah, soon
I'd break your heart to go a-roaming,
And chasing shadows of the moon
    Think never once of homing.

Why will you wring my breast with tears?
Tears will not quench the Wander-fever.
Why will you fill my soul with fears
    When I will go for ever?

I whom the Earth's green passions move
Have put away all passions human  .  .  .
I will not love!  .  .  I *dare* not love  .  .
    Turn by your eyes, White Woman.

## VI

I went far and cold
Over upland wold
Where the story of spring's breathing
Scarcely yet was told.
Shifting monotone
Of the pale wind's moan
Through my hair at dusk went wreathing,
And I walked alone.

Far below and far
Where the homesteads are
One small ruddy candle twinkled,
Warmer than a star.
When the day was gone,
Softly one by one
Homing-lights the valley sprinkled  .  .  .
And I wandered on.

# KING LAURIN'S GARDEN

*(A Styrian Peasant-Girl Dreams at her Wheel)*

King Laurin has a garden of roses
Where warm sweet odours do idly flow
Wave upon wave through the charmèd air  .  .  .
It is sin to wish for the garden of roses
In the heart of wild mountains where no men go.

Laurin is king of a rosy garden.
The lure of the roses is rare, O rare!
They tremble and brighten and throb and glow  .  .  .
I may not think of King Laurin's garden.
A danger, they tell me, for maids is there.

There are four high gates to the garden of roses,
For the treasure of bloom a golden guard,
A precious cup for the rose-wine red.
O the golden gates of the garden of roses!
They are bright and beautiful, tall and barred.

There is no strong wall round the rosy garden;
From gate to gate runs a woven thread,
Yellow and silken and fine, for ward.
Who snaps the ward of the rosy garden
With his hand and his foot shall he pay, 'tis said.

# KING LAURIN'S GARDEN

Laurin who rules the garden of roses
Is an elf-king, therefore he has no soul.
(*The good priest shudders at Laurin's name.*)
Poor soulless elf of the garden of roses!
Shall I pray for King Laurin at Vesper-toll?

They say no prayers in the rosy garden
Where life is the flash of a fragrant flame
Like the heart of a flower on fire: the whole
Of forbidden sweet is the rosy garden
I may not think of and feel no shame.

For in King Laurin's garden of roses
Waking thought shall be stilled asleep,
And the still heart dream itself half-awake   .   .   .
O the soft, soft dreams of the garden of roses!
They creep . . . (*I look not*) . . . but they steal and

Laurin the king of the rosy garden
Has a magic girdle that none can break.
It makes the pulse of his life to leap
With twelve men's strength.   In the rosy garden
He is feared and feared for the girdle's sake.

Laurin the king of the garden of roses
Has a magic crown where strange birds so sing
That resistance and doubt by their song once kissed
Melt into trance.   In the garden of roses
He is loved and loved for his crowned bird-ring.

# KING LAURIN'S GARDEN

Laurin the king of the rosy garden
Has a magic cloak the colour of mist,
And he goes invisibly wandering
Far from the bourne of the rosy garden
Like a cloud of pearl and of amethyst.

He seeks a bride for his garden of roses,
For the soulless spirit a human girl  .  .  .
(*The priest bids me wear my cross and pray*)  .  .  .
He will bear her back to his garden of roses
In the mist of his magic grey-and-pearl.

Kunhild was borne to the rosy garden,
The sister of Dietrich of Bern, one day.
A fair green mead and a cloud's dim swirl,
And Kunhild awoke in the rosy garden  .  .  .
But she stood by a linden-tree first, they say.

.        .        .        .

*King Laurin has a garden of roses*
*Full of warm odours*  .  .  .  I'll sit and spin
As my Mother bids me  .  .  .  *O wine-red glow*
*Of half-waked dreams in the garden of roses*  .  .  .
Spin, wheel!  .  .  .  *fine thread, bright like silk, and th*

*A grey mist steals from the rosy garden*
*In the heart of wild mountains where no men go*  .  .  .
To think of the garden they say is sin—
I'll dream no more of King Laurin's garden  .  .  .
*See! in our meadow green lindens grow*  .  .  .

# THE MYSTERIOUS FOREST

I stood on the verge of the mysterious forest,
Sunlight lay behind me on the meadows,
But all the world of the mysterious forest
Was a world of wraiths and shadows.

The dim trees beckoned, beckoned with their branches,
I said: "The sun's behind me on the meadows."
A dim voice calling, calling through the branches
From the world of wraiths and shadows.

I saw a pale young Queen, her eyes were mournful,
Steal ghostwise . . . is the sun yet on the meadows? .
More phantoms passed and all their eyes were mournful
In the world of wraiths and shadows.

I see a blue light in the mysterious forest,
The cold night lies behind me on the meadows.
The branches beckon in the mysterious forest . . .
They beckon, beckon, beckon, call and beckon
From the world of wraiths and shadows.

# THE OLD GREY QUEEN

The Princess looked from the old grey tower;
She was a-weary of being there.
She wore no crown but her own gold hair,
And the old grey Queen had shut her there,
    She was so like a flower.

" The young King's-Son comes over the sea
  From the West," said the Queen who was grey and old.
" In an unlit hall were not grey as gold?
  In an unlit hall what are young and old?
      We'll greet i' the dark," said she.

The Princess looked from the old grey tower  .  .  .
Lo! a milk-white sail on the sunlit ocean.
Fluttered her heart to its fluttering motion,
And the King's-Son looked from the golden ocean  .  .
    She was so like a flower.

" Why do the grey seas break and boom?
  And why is the starless dusk so grey?
  And why does the young King's-Son delay?
  Shall I," said the Queen who was old and grey,
      " Sit all night i' the gloom? "

# THE OLD GREY QUEEN

The grey seas broke on an empty tower
Like pain that knocks on an empty breast.
Lo! a milk-white sail that flew the crest
Of Love and of Youth met breast to breast
Melted away in the golden West  .   .   .

The old grey Queen beat her empty breast
  "She was so like a flower."

# THE QUEST

A Knight rides forth upon a Quest,
And his young Squire follows after ;
The Knight's eyes dwell on a star's white crest,
And the Squire's eyes dwell on laughter.

" What of the Quest that claims our swords ? "
The young Squire asks his master.
The Knight says, " 'Tis too high for words,"
And they speed their horses faster.

A beggar hails them : "Alms ! alms, Sir Knight,
Or loose my life with your dagger ! "
The Knight sees only a star's white light,
And the Squire's purse pays the beggar.

A sturdy robber the highroad bars :
" Sir Knight, our debts we'll settle ! "
The Knight hears only the song of stars,
And the Squire's blade wins the battle.

A lady looks from a castle wall :
" Sir Knight, in pity stay thee !
Untrammel me who lie here in thrall,
And I in love will pay thee."

# THE QUEST

The Knight is set on a goal heaven-high
Where a silver star is risen,
And the young Squire it is springs by
To free the maid from prison.

" Take, good Sir Knight, my pleasure and pride,
The meed of valiant striving!
Here wait the lips of your glad bride
Whose name is Joy-of-Living."

Starward, starward the rapt Knight goes,
The star's true image missing.
The lady laughs like a lovely rose
And the Squire's lips do the kissing.

" What, boy, are you my love doth woo?
What's he that would not woo it?"
" He's John-a-Dreams-o'-Dering-do,
And I'm Dick-up-an'-Do-it."

# THE UNSPOKEN WORD

### THE MAN'S SIDE

Two years I have lived in a dream
And have dared not to end it—
Owned wealth in a measure supreme
And been fearful to spend it.

You, woman of beauty and love
In such noble wise fashioned,
Are my dreams and my rich treasure-trove.
I am shamed that, impassioned,

In secret I levy demands
Upon more than you've given—
Crave yourself, heart and soul, eyes and hands,
Which in sum make up heaven.

Unconscious of aught, through these days
You have let me be near you,
Knowing not how your thousand sweet ways
Only serve to endear you

To all in your orbit who move,
In such innocence wronging
As friendship what really is love
And unsatisfied longing.

26

# THE UNSPOKEN WORD

Yet, your friendship—to be just your friend—
So caps love in another,
That I would my love, burned to its end,
In its own smoke might smother,

Lest I in an outbreak one day
Ask of friendship aught stronger—
When you may forbid me to say
Even " friend " any longer.

So I come in the old way and go,
While my heart's quickened beatings
Are hidden, and you never know
What I glean from our meetings;

How a word,  a look even, which seems
So unconsciously meted,
Builds new dreams on the wreckage of dreams
That were never completed.

You once dropped a flower—did not see
That I hid in my bosom
What was more than Golconda to me,
And to you a bruised blossom.

Ten seconds I once held your hand
While you pulled from the river
A lily.  Could you understand
Why my own hand should quiver?

# THE UNSPOKEN WORD

Small matters these things you account
Who so lightly diffuse them,
But to all my life's joy they amount --
And my fear is, to lose them.

One day, when your eyes are still kind
And your voice is still tender,
I shall slip the control of my mind,
All my future surrender,

Obeying the primal desire
To fall down and adore you,
And outpour in one instant of fire
All the love I have for you.

'Twill be death, and far worse, at your feet
When my lips cease to blunder
And I look up your dear eyes to meet
Overrunning with wonder.

Thereafter—what? Nothing, I fear—
Even dreams will have vanished
When I by my act from your sphere
Shall for ever be banished.

Dear, that is the moment I dread—
When you hear my confession,
When the word I withhold has been said
And my love finds expression ;

## THE UNSPOKEN WORD

But till then (and God knows how I seek
To postpone and postpone it),
Till my love grows too strong, lips too weak
To much longer disown it,

I shall come, if I may, day by day,
My small gleanings to gather,
While you think of me—how shall we say?
As a brother or father;

And you never will guess, till you learn
From a heart brimming over,
That I've met you at every turn
As a passionate lover.


### THE WOMAN'S SIDE

How long will you hold back, belov'd?   How long
Leave the supreme, the final word unspoken?
The barrier of silence hold unbroken?
    Men—you, too, being a man—have called you strong,
A doer of big deeds, great acts.   But they are wrong.

· You lack in courage.   I, being woman, know
    How often woman shapes man's enterprises,
    Cloaking her work in manifold disguises
    Lest he should chafe too large a debt to owe—
Strikes every blow up to the very hundredth blow

# THE UNSPOKEN WORD

That shall at last resolve, achieve, complete
The foregone nine-and-ninety.   This, grown wiser,
She leaves with him for fear he should despise her.
*He* wins the credit for the final feat—
Thought of *his* triumph, not hers, made all her toiling sweet.

Belov'd, how long before you understand?
Why, I have known two years you were my lover,
That all my being to yours was given over!
The thing your heart most yearns for lies at hand
Awaiting only this, that you shall make demand.

Have I not worked for all betwixt us two
Since first I saw your love spring into being,
And you became too faint of heart for seeing
That the one peach you longed to garner grew,
Ripened, and mellowed here only for you, for you?

You would have drawn abashed from out my life
Had I permitted; it became *my* mission
To bring the golden moment to fruition
Through, ah, how many hours of wistful strife
With you, who guessed not, even, the tender struggle rife

Between us.   When I met you with a smile,
"Love's not for me," you thought, "yet while she kindly
Still looks and speaks, I'll stay."   And went thus blindly
Taking for innocence what sprang from guile
That I might hold you by me just a little while.

# THE UNSPOKEN WORD

The day I dropped a flower upon the path,
Did you not know it was the thing I aimed for
When you behind me loitered (somewhat lamed for
A good excuse), secured it free from scath
And hid it close, to reap therefrom love's aftermath

In hours when I was absent?   Why, I *meant*,
Belov'd, that you should have this one flower-treasure
(Stolen, you thought!) out of my heart's full measure—
Meant that your solitary nights be spent
Cheek to its petals pressed where all my love lay pent.

And then, the day you helped me from the boat,
" It is but chance," you thought, " I hold her fingers
In mine past custom's limit, while she lingers
To cull the waterlily there afloat."
It was not chance, belov'd.   And still you would not note.

I have done all a woman may do, dear,
With eyes and hands and tones of voice have spoken,
In all but words have given you the token
And seal of love.   What is it then you fear?
Can you not take one step, the goal being now so near?

Just the last word to utter, just the last
Step to be taken—it is very little!
Can you believe Love's structure is so brittle?
All I have builded in these two years past
Fall tottering at one word?   It is of stronger cast.

# THE UNSPOKEN WORD

You would not have me speak.   That part is yours.
My share is finished and I wait for you now.
The time to act has come—what will you do now?
Dear, even I'd say the word that all ensures
But that were more than love itself of love endures.

I had to spend my strength when you were weak,
Be guide along the road from its beginning
To the last barrier.   Am I worth the winning?
But *you* must turn the key.   It will not creak.
Beloved, I am waiting still   .   .   .   will you not speak?

# IN THE OCULIST'S ANTEROOM

## I

Not to be able to see ! . . .
Almost as well not be.
And that man in there in his single hand
Holds all God's light,
Or just so much, you understand,
As may be drunk in by another's sight—
Dear God, will he give the light to me ?

Or will a fathomless night
Drop its veil across the sight
Of my straining eyes, to become mere husks
Whence the kernel slips,
Knowing none of God's dawns and only God's dusks . . .
That man has them all at his finger-tips.
Dear God ! will he clear the dusk from the light ?

## II

He has spoken.  The man with his cold voice has spoken.
The seal of suspense lies here shattered and broken,
*And I know* . . . And I know
What the coming years hold which an hour since were dumb
    to me—
God ! how precious the jewel of your light has become to me
Where's my hat ?  Let me go.

33

C

## LITTLE DREAM-BROTHER.

Little dream-brother that died
When I was not a year out of heaven,
I heard you when you tried
To come to me yestereven.

As I lay in bed
Midway 'twixt nothingness and waking,
I heard the window shaking
And the beat of wings upon the pane.
" It is not the rain,
  But my little dream-brother out there," I said.

I turned in bed :
" Come in, little dream-brother."
" I can only come in by the gates of sleep
  And by no other.
  Through the niche of the tiniest dream I can creep
  Sleep, sister, do sleep," you said.

And so through the night we waited—
You on the window-threshold there
In the wet windy weather,
And I abed—with breath bated,
Just to catch the first moment of sleep unaware
And fly kissing together.

But sleep would not come till seven,
When the shivering day
Looked up all chilly and grey.
" Creep into bed,
Little dream-brother, under my arm
And I'll keep you warm."
But you shook your head :
" It's bed-time in heaven,
Sister.   Goodbye," you said.

There was not a whole year between you
And me, little dream-brother.
I cannot remember even to have seen you
And now I might be your mother.

# FAUST AND MARGARET

"Devil," he said, "Love's Heaven—
 Shall man not therefor lose his soul?"

. . . . . .

"God," she whispered, "is Love Heaven?
 Is Heaven a place of dole?"

*(And so she gave his Heaven to the man*
*Because the man did crave it.*
*And so because she never asked Hell's ban*
*He gave it.)*

"Devil!" he said, "Love's Hell!
 Man's wild-beast-thirst, how slake it?
 Take the tenderest thing, thus—thus!
 Passion-torture it a spell,
 And break it!"

. . . . . .

"God," she whispered, "Love is Heaven.
 Love's not what Love is made for us,
 But what we make it."

*(And so her dead soul found what it had given,*
*And what he builded, there his damned soul ended.*
*And do you think that either Hell or Heaven*
*These sinners' suffering-on-earth amended?)*

# DREAM-SHIPS

I set my dream-ships floating
Upon the tides of sleep.
Beneath whose moving waters
Unfathomed currents creep;

And one was made of roses
With flowering mast and spars,
And one was made of music,
And one was made of stars:

One was all joy and sorrow
Made from my own heart-strings,
And one was like a cradle
With sails like angels' wings.

O little ships that wander
All lonely on the deep,
And only come to haven
Upon the tides of sleep.

# THE MORAL

The youth cried in anguish: "God,
My life is bowed down beneath
Its woe! I am no mere clod—
There's fire in my blood and breath.

"You, Who made me of flesh, not stone,
Of quivering tissues—dare
You leave me to face alone
A grief past my strength to bear?

"Life might be veriest heaven,
Life can be veriest hell—
In *Your* hands rests what is given.
God, I hold You responsible!"

Then the man who was growing grey
Observed: "In an idle mood
God blew bubbles one day
And loosed the glistening brood

On the welkin, one by one—
Myriads of worlds they sped:
There were planets and moon and sun,
And one was the globe we tread.

# THE MORAL

Then the Spirit that Nullifies,
Men term Death, asked : "How long?" (One fears
God shrugged.)  "While I blink my eyes—
Shall we say a billion years?"

.     .     .     .     .     .

The youth on the fable broke,
And scorn in his accents ran :
"What is all this to me?  I spoke
To God of *Myself*, old man."

# COLOUR-TONES

## I

A visionary filmy sheen
Scarce palpable of silver-green
Limns barren furrow and bare branch.
One month more, and the welcoming
Gates o' the world will open wide
To let the full deep vernal tide
Sweep overland, an avalanche
Of green, absorbing in its rush
This silver-misty verdure . . . Hush!
This is the old earth's dream of Spring.

## II

In Cobham woods the bluebells run
Celestial rillets, streams and rivers,
Or else a purple lake they lie,
Or little azure pool ;
The blue flood shimmers in the sun
Or under the wind's breathing shivers,
While drops cerulean-tincted spill
Among the grass. Then very still
The dim sweet waters grow and cool
Like shadows of the sky.

# COLOUR-TONES

## III

The yellow light of daffodils
The lawns beneath the fruit-trees fills,
The yellow light of early spring
Swims in the shining upper air,
And all about the fragrant fair
Blossoming boughs of sunlit white
Like clouds of heavenly incense swing
'Twixt yellow light and yellow light.

# FROM AN OLD GARDEN

## OUTSIDE

Trees have grown to the edge of the gate
Where grey-bearded lichens cling;
The greenwoods stand in a ring,
Holding the garden-pearl in their centre
A jewel inviolate.
Heart of mine, shall we enter?

There is a charm of sleep in the air,
Weft of Time's humming loom.
There in the green half-gloom
I think some intangible spirit hovers  .  .  .
They say the dim wraiths dwell there
Of countless, long-dead lovers.

Warp of sleep and woof of love:
The flush of a live rose glows
By the pallid death of the rose,
A song next the hush that stilled its numbers:
Such is the web Time wove.
Dare we disturb their slumbers?

We stand on the outskirts, you and I—
Shall we not venture in?
They will condone the sin,
Those dim, dead lovers, will smile and pardon,
For our honeymoon hangs in the sky.
Heart of mine, into the garden!

# FROM AN OLD GARDEN

## INSIDE

You and I here!
Shut the gate behind us.
Nothing to fear
And none to find us.
We are all the world, dear!

'Tis a cloister of dreams,
This dear old garden;
The sundial seems
To stand as their warden.
How Love's star gleams!

We'll sup on the rose,
Our tent is this willow—
Lie close, Love, close!
There's grass for our pillow.
How Love's star glows!

You and I here
And the world behind us!
Nothing to fear
And none to find us—
Shut the gate, dear.

43

# FROM AN OLD GARDEN

## FLOW'R AND SONG

Song and flow'r and flow'r and song,
So soothed the summer drifts along :
    Within our hearts a flow'r
    Unfolding hour by hour,
    While a song half-concious slips
    Over my dear one's lips.
Flow'r and song and song and flow'r,
So filled runs by each swift, sweet hour :
    Close to my breast you twine
    Your flow'r-lips laid on mine,
    And I catch before we part
    The song-beats of your heart.
Flow'r and song in our garden-close
Like wedded lovers have grown one word.
I could weave you a wreath from the notes of that bird,
And pluck you a song from the heart of this rose.

## DWELLERS IN THE GARDEN

    Who dwelt here of old ?
Hush ! If I lift from the misty years
The veil of dead smiles and forgotten tears,
I think I can picture a little maid
    Crowned with plaits of gold,
Passing alone down each green arcade
    While the sundial told
In silence its hours of shine and shade.

## FROM AN OLD GARDEN

Young she was as the peep of dawn,
And as a year-old dappled fawn
Was shy and tender and innocent.
And all her days were in waiting spent
Amongst her flowers in a day-dream she
Builded herself.   So continuously
In waiting and waiting the days went by—
We know what she waited, love, you and I.
The flowers had nothing to teach to her—
In her sleep she could hear the grasses stir,
She had secrets with every rose in the place,
The lilies kept smiles for her lily-face,
She could think their thoughts and utter their speech,
Had a sister's tender look for each,
And knew why the trailing clematis
Dropped on the sundial a purple kiss —
As surely as we know why, she knew.
And so in her house of dreams she grew,
And so the star-lighted nights slipped by.
We know what she waited for—you and I—
  Who dwelt here of old.
  There's her tale half-told.

  What more to unfold?
When he came at last did they ride away,
Or, day succeeding each happy day,
Did they stay with two heartfuls of love to brim
The garden wherein she had waited him?

## FROM AN OLD GARDEN

Well, this I know.   If they stayed  or went,
After their term of life was spent
They returned to roam by her lily-pond,
On to the rosery set beyond,
Haunt her favourite paths and nooks,
Re-read the fairy-tales which her books,
The flowers, had yielded her in such store
When he was the hero of all their lore.
Hand in hand they go as of old,
    He brave and bold,
    She crowned with gold.

Ah, love, they are neither the first nor last !
For all of those, having loved and passed,
In spirit come back when their dust is cold,
    Who dwelt here of old.


## A ROSE-SONG

Oh, what a realm, what a riot of roses !
Here we stand
Right in the heart of a great rose-land !
Over our head the blossom-world closes,
Under our feet—
Walls, ceil and carpet are flowery-sweet.

# FROM AN OLD GARDEN

Snowy and crimson and pink and golden
Twine and trail,
Vivid as life is, as death is, pale.
Here they bloom as they bloomed in olden
Days when we
Were unborn shades, and the shades that be

Had right in these grounds to resent intrusion.
Now you and I
Jealously cherish our privacy.
How came these roses by their profusion,
Tier on tier
Of bloom on bloom running uncurb'd here?

I think I can guess what they would answer,
Whence they came,
Pallid petal and flower of flame,
Inscribed with such lore as the old romancer
Of Italy
Left the world to make love-songs by.

We are born, these pink roses say, of kisses,
,Dye of the blush.
What though time's passage their soft lisp hush?
The seeds were scattered of lovers' blisses,
And year by year
We renew thier tender caresses here.

# FROM AN OLD GARDEN

We are born of joy, say these petals yellow,
Tinge of delight.
What though love's sunshine be lapped in night?
We, sprung from its seeds, rich-toned and mellow,
Perpetuate
The days when the orbit of love waxed great.

We are born, these red ones say, of passion,
Flush of the heart.
What though the sound of love's steps depart?
The seeds were sown, and we in this fashion
Immortalize
Remembrance thereof in the heart's own dyes.

We are born, say these snow-white blooms, of the spirit,
Children of death.
What is the ceasing of mere life-breath?
Love is sustained by its own pure merit,
Its memory
Renewed and renewed to infinity.

Belov'd, we are adding to these rose-bowers.
When we have passed
Here our hearts' treasure will lie amassed.
Pink, gold, crimson and snowy flowers,
Thus and thus,
To the limit of time will bloom for us.

48

# FROM AN OLD GARDEN

## BY THE FOUNTAIN

Come down, dear, to the fountain's pool with me,
And help me guess how long since last it tinkled
And trickled out thin streams of minstrelsy—

How long since last the grass with pearls it sprinkled.
It was yet young the day it fell asleep,
For time has left its glassy face unwrinkled.

Ah, could we where the shadows lie most deep
Peering discern the dear forgotten faces
Of girls who o'er the brink were wont to peep,

With shy eyes seeking in the depths the graces
Made dear and lovely to them by love's praise.
Can all have passed away and left no traces?

They dreamed, as we too dream, through summer days,
And hid their white thoughts in such water-lilies
As float here now, Flowers do not change their ways.

Ah, love, to-day the lucent water still is
As tho' no rosy finger-tips had dipped
And dabbled it, and hushed the fountain's rill is.

49

D

# FROM AN OLD GARDEN

Their feet across the velvet greensward tripped,
Their bosoms pressed the crumbling grey-stone basin,
They fed the ruddy goldfish laughing-lipped  .  .  .

Is not one left?   Look, look !   I seem to trace in
The murky deeps some shape of hoary carp—
Too late ! for now I only see your face in

The water, smiling questions.   He was sharp,
That king-fish, but I caught his gold crown's glimmer . .
Oh, fountain, tune again for us your harp,

Fling through the air for us your diamond shimmer
Of spray.   Two new young lovers seek your shrine.
Those loves of old with years grow fainter, dimmer,

But ours is warm and living and divine,
And time has not yet breathed upon its lustre,
And I am hers and she is all of mine !

And here we kneel where once old loves would muster,
Shut in the lilies one new secret up,
And add her image to the beauty-cluster
Of those whose eyes lie mirrored in your cup.

# FROM AN OLD GARDEN

## TIME AND LOVE

Old sundial, you stand here for Time :
For Love, the vine that round your base
Its tendrils twines, and dares to climb
And lay one flower-capped spray in grace
Without the asking on your cold
Unsmiling and unfrowning face.
Yet, sundial, even Time may mould.
In years to come the foot shall stumble
Upon your shattered ruins where
This vine will flourish still, as rare,
As fresh, as fragrant as of old.
      Love will not crumble.

Kisses have worn your stones away,
Lov'd lips you did not pulse beneath ;
Dropt tears have hastened your decay
And brought you one step nigher death ;
And you have heard, unthrilled, unmoved,
The music of Love's golden breath
And seen the light in eyes that loved.
You think you hold the core and kernel
Of all the world beneath your crust,
Old dial?  But when you lie in dust,
This vine will bloom, strong, green, and proved.
      Love is eternal.

# FROM AN OLD GARDEN

## RIFLED FLOWERS

Why is the lily's cheek waxen with grief ?
A brown-and-gold thief
Dived down to her core
And burgled her store.
Bowed with her sweetness she saw him depart,
But her soul was too pure to complain.
Dear, drop a kiss in her heart
And make the sweet lily all honey again.

Why does the fox-glove droop low, bell and leaf?
A silver-winged thief
Who delved in her pollen
With gold powder swollen
Fled in new blossoms her wealth to disburse
And left her not one yellow grain.
Sweet, blow a kiss in her purse
And fill the dear fox-glove with treasure again.

# FROM AN OLD GARDEN

## FAIRY-TIME

Lie very still, love, where I fold
You close : the clocks strike fairy-time.
The thin, sweet tinkle of their chime
Is like a thread of gold
Woven through the heart of night
For our delight.
And following the elfin call
Faint noises, half-tones, rise and fall—
The whirr and flit of fairy wings
Pass and re-pass,
And we can hear among the grass
Musicians tune their buzzing strings,
And small feet tapping on the ground
The measures of a fairy round.
Out of the roses stream wee elves,
Sweet peas are fairies in themselves,
And myriad water-sprites
From dreaming water-lilies rise,
Such glistening, ephemeral mites,
Flashing like spray across our eyes.
Watch how all whirl, dissolve, and mix
Again, foot it so daintily,
Play such quaint, pretty tricks—
Some on wild moths go riding by,

FROM AN OLD GARDEN

Breaking them in with rein and bit
Of gossamer : some lurk and flit,
Making pretence at hide and-seek
Behind the daisies, laugh and peek
Like children : disregarding rules,
Play leap-frog with the spotted stools
Of fungus, each night newly-sprung
For them to sport among  .  .  .
Suddenly all grow hushed with awe—
Come closer, dear !
The voice of one who broke the law
Of Fairyland sounds harsh and near,
And overhead a dark shape flies.
Bound in a hollow oak by day
He, like the wizard Merlin, lies,
But is condemned to pass the night
In restless flight
Until the dawn looms grey  .  .  .  .
There ! he has passed.   And in a trice
They all forget him, joining hands
Once more in glittering, laughing bands,
Employing every strange device
And twist and twirl
And mazy whirl
To build their graceful, freakish dance—
Like moonbeam motes they glide and glance
Under the starshine.   Seize this chance

## FROM AN OLD GARDEN

Of watching them.   To-morrow we
No trace shall see
Of all their revels save—who knows ?—
A broken toadstool, or the spun
Fine silken spider's web undone,
The shattered petals of a rose
Torn in the careless frolic, or
The bloom brushed from some untamed wing
Of moth, and on their dancing-floor
Staining the grass a bright green ring.
Lie close, and let us look our fill
To-night.   Be very still.


## THE WANING YEAR

Two little things, dear, I have seen
To-day that overflowed my breast with sorrow—
We may not stay here many another morrow.

Amongst the leafage, by its green
Still-living sisters tenderly enfolden,
I saw one single leaf grown dry and golden.

And down the alleys of the rose
Passing, I saw one lightly breathed-on blossom
Fall instantly deflowered to earth's brown bosom.

Compassionate summer ere she goes
Strikes tender notes surcharged with wistful warnings .
Dear heart, we must begone ere many mornings.

55

## SHADOWS

We thought we were here alone,
Had spent our summer of love
By all other hearts unknown,
Of all other eyes unseen—
But something came to disprove
Last night what we thought had been.

The shadows fell one by one—
We have watched them fall before
And fancied ourselves alone ;
But they seemed to waver and move
Last night, and to wander o'er
Our green-tented couch of love.

You were asleep, and I
Would not disturb your dreams
Lest the shadowy shapes should fly.
I saw them gather and mount
In ever-increasing streams—
More lovers than I could count.

They circled around our bed
And watched us a little while
From the sides and foot and head ;
And some of that shadow-band
Were wistful, and some would smile,
But all seemed to understand.

## FROM AN OLD GARDEN

Then I felt light fingers twine
In my hair, and soft breath enwreathe
My brow  .  .  .  lips were laid to mine  .  .
But none of the hands was this,
Nor the breath the breath you breathe,
The kissess were not your kiss.

Then  .  .  .  you turned on your side to press
More close with the smile that slips
From its hiding at my caress,
And you breathed my name in my ear
As though I had kissed your lips  .  .  .
.But I had not kissed you, dear.


## THE LAST NIGHT

Well, is it done ?  is it over ?
Three months in these groves I have been your lover,
Added my voice to the echoing chorus
    Of those who loved here before us.

We have pressed the paths made sweet
By the pressure of bygone lovers' feet,
Have lain amid flowerless violet-beds
·   Where they laid their happy heads ;

    We have flung a red-rose petal
On the glass of the pond and watched it settle,
Then drift like a boat down one of her streams
    With our cargo of hopes and dreams.

# FROM AN OLD GARDEN

So many have come and gone,
Have done the things which we two have done:
Have leaned in revery sweet and solemn,
    Hands laced, on the sundial's column:

Have found their three months as brief
As the life of a blade of grass, a leaf—
As eternal, too, as the leafage is
    Have found their three months of bliss.

For us it is finished and over.
Our three months are spent when as lover and lover
We may roam these groves. But to-night we are
        nearest,
    This being our last night, dearest,

The spirits of those who wander
Near our lily-pond, by our sundial yonder,
In our rose-realm  .  .  .  Farewells are not easily
        spoken,
    So their silence remains unbroken.

But I see through a mist of tears
This garden after a million years,
Where two shades more move eternally  .  .  .
    Heart of mine, they are you and I.

# A SHEAF OF NATURE-SONGS

## (Overstrand, 1905.)

### I

They were gathered up in the moods
Which I found in the solitudes
Of the shore and the fields and the woods,
Of the dawn and the noon and the even,
Of the earth and the sea and of heaven.
And some lack rhythm and metre,
And none of the songs is sweeter,
Or as sweet (by the infinite span
Which divides the work of man
From the work of his God), as the thing
Which was the fountain and spring
Whence my heart drew its need to sing.
But because wherever I went
Much song in my heart was pent:
Because the sea and the sky
Filled my breast with such melody:
Because the woodlands and all
God's earth became musical
As they entered into my soul:
ᐧBecause I captured the whole
Of Nature for my possession:
I sang just to find expression
For the joy and the love and the pride of it—
Else all song in me might have died of it.

59

## II

The infinite sky overhead
And on the horizon
The infinite sea.
Green billowing grass for my bed—
At last I am out of my prison
And free!

An insect creeps over my page,
An infinite mite
With all life folded under its wings.
I am of no sex, of no age,
Here out of sight
Of the world, all alone with God's infinite things.

Oh, the world of small leafage
Peopling the bank where I lean,
And the one white daisy
With its wisdom of things supernal.
They live out their brief age,
Brief but eternal,
And time itself recedes and grows hazy
In this little infinite world of green.

## A SHEAF OF NATURE-SONGS

Behind me the copse
Like a round cup dips
Filled with a pool of soft shadows,
And to me in the meadows
One shy bird-voice from the tree-top drips
And into the hollow of shadows it melts and drops.

They are all around me
And all above me,
Half-seen, half-heard,
Flower and leaf and insect and bird,
Wild, timid creatures,
Simple and friendly and shy;
And so still I lie
Where they have found me
That I think in time they may learn to love me,
For they are Nature's
And so am I.

One by one she unfolds each feature,
The Infinite Mother
To her child.
There was a new bird-call,
And there was another !
I too shall learn to grow simple and shy and wild  .  .
Only Nature and Nature and nothing but Nature,
And I alone in the heart of it all.

## III

They who dwell in the southlands say,
Little green England of mine, that you
Are misty and colourless, cold and grey.
    If it be true
And they can know it who dwell afar,
You only are grey as diamonds are.

To-day in the warm soft evening light
You are a zone of delicate tints ;
On the rim of the sea the sun is bright,
    And shoots and glints
Sparkles of gold through its splendid blue.
Who say you are colourless know not you.

Opal gleams on the sunset sky
Where a wave of the liquid sapphire flows ;
One bright cloud on its flood drifts by
    Of pearl and rose ;
The air is radiant and crystalline
As rare jewels delved from a fairy mine.

# A SHEAF OF NATURE-SONGS

A breeze just shivers the green of the corn
And sweeps it into a silver sea ;
Infinite sensitive shades new-born
    On hill and lea
Over the land's lap flit and pass
Like elusive tints in Venetian glass

Nature has painted you in pastel,
You are her palette of tender hues,
Little green England of mine, where dwell
    Change, and infuse,
The million lights of the polar-star,
And you only are grey as diamonds are.

## IV

If I could unravel
The music of the grass,
Beyond those confines travel
Which mortals cannot pass,
I think that I should capture all
The secret of things musical—
All music ever will be, and all it ever was.

Ear close to earth inclining
I hear her wordless song
Of threads past man's divining
Woven the grass among.
Beneath these fragrant, tangled weeds
She sings the strain to which her seeds
March into life, push upward to heaven, and grow strong.

Then like a voice replying
Follows her cradle-croon
Lulling tired things that, dying,
Back to their Mother swoon.
For where the worlds of grasses spring
Both life and death their choral sing,
The spheres' eternal roundel circling an afternoon.

# A SHEAF OF NATURE-SONGS

The music of existence
Moves underneath my ear—
From how remote a distance
Comes that which sounds so near!
Could I the human barrier pass
By the fine measure of one grass
I then might comprehend what now I only hear.

There's such melodious stirring
Of hidden, secret things,
There's such harmonious whirring
Of faint mysterious wings;
And underneath this leaf is curled
The song, I think, of all the world—
Up-turned, should I discover the seed from which
    springs?

If I could unravel
The music of the grass,
Beyond those confines travel
Which mortals cannot pass,
I think that I should capture all
The secret of things musical—
All music ever will be, and all it ever was.

E

V

Hark!
It is afternoon,
Yet that must be a lark.
No other bird flies up so high
And shakes its sparkling spray of song
Through the grey clouds in the sky,
No other bird has just that thrilling
Note in trilling,
Or can sustain so long
Its liquid flood of mirth:
As rare a boon
To thirsty ears as God's dew is to earth.
Yet it is afternoon.
I thought the larks, all scorning
The jaded hours, sang only in the morning.
And I, whose first flushed youth is going,
Who watch the swift noon growing
Upon me, hour by hour,
Feeling that I must always stand apart
From earth's sweet singers, because I lacked the pow'r
To loose the morning song-burst from my heart—
Oh, songster of the mellowing hour of day,
Shall I, too, late or soon,
Learn from your throat the way
To loose my power of song even in my afternoon?

## VI

The day was a lifeless day.
Under a tree I lay
And round me its branches bent
Touching the earth like a tent.
There was no stir of breeze;
I was shut in with trees,
Locked from the world by these;
Dead leaves were piled on the ground,
And the forest lay in a swound,
Throbbed with nor pulse nor breath,
And I thought: "It is waiting Death."
So I lay there, still and oppressed,
While the silence grew in my breast.

Presently as I lay
I heard from far away
Little pattering feet
Over the dry leaves beat;
Tripping along pell-mell,
Thicker and faster they fell
Than tongue could count or tell.

And I fancied the birds and deer
And rabbits, too awed for fear,
Were creeping my aid to plead
Impelled by our common need—
Till into my sheltered place
One raindrop splashed on my face.

I lay there tented and dry
While the dews, dropped out of the sky,
Made music upon the sheaves
Of last year's stacked-up leaves—
No steps of wild things that trod,
But the whispering voice of God
In grave commune with the sod,
Messenger-angels rife
With words not of Death but Life,
Bidding the old brown Earth
Prepare for her great re-birth
And look to Heaven in pride
Renewed and revivified.

Then I heard far under the soil
The seedlings stir and toil,
And blade and bulb and root
Put forth each one new shoot,

And I felt deep down and deep
A million pulses leap
Out of their term of sleep,
And I thought the acorn spoke
With the voice of the full-grown oak,
And the cone wore the crown divine
Of the red-stemmed, crested pine,
And the haw held all the blush
And bloom of the wild-rose bush.

What helped these young things to grow?
Dead leaves of a year ago,
Leaves heaped up in their crowds
And spread like funeral-shrouds;
Yet life sprang out of their death
As the blade slips out of its sheath,
Life was fostered beneath
The leaves here rotting away
And emerged from their decay.
Are all things that seem to die
Renewed to infinity,
And the bodies and souls of men
Made and re-made again?

With the scent of the rain-wet loam
In my nostrils, I turned me home.

## VII

I lay on the shore beside the sea,
And the young moon climbed the hill of the sky
And paused a space to look down on me
    Alone with my misery.

Then on the fallow blue fields above
The young moon sowed its seed of stars ;
Light gleamed from the mirror of her named Love
    And flashed from the shield of Mars.

The stars sprang up from the silver seed
Wherever that silver sower trod.
Through the windows of heaven watching my need
    I knew them the eyes of God.

Little blue waves with blown foam capped
Crept on the solitary shore
Which the sea's white lips still licked and lapped
    For ever and evermore.

The silver moon waxed strong and older ;
I thought I saw it stop to fling
A silver sick'e over its shoulder
    And commence its harvesting.

The strong moon ploughed through the fields of heaven,
Its eternal labour but half-begun.
My breast dropped its load of earthy leaven
    As the stars dropped one by one.

I had sat there hugging my trivial cross,
My infinitesimal mortal pains,
Reckoning up how my mortal loss
    Outmeasured my mortal gains.

I saw the moon reaping God's blue fields
Night after night sown thick with seeds.
I saw the crop which God's harvest yields
    Not in men's dreams, but deeds.

The old moon climbed down the hill of the sky,
The strong young day flashed up in flame.
The moon dropped into the sea, and I
    Bowed down my head in shame.

# APOLLO IN PHERAE

*Asklepios! dead son! Asklepios!*

I was a God.  I am a God.  I tend
Admetos' flocks upon the meek green earth,
And sun-fires course in all the veins of me.
I watch mild sheep a-browse in tame, sweet pastures
Or dipping in quiet waters.   Yesterday
I blazed the heavenly arc from east to west;
Men saw me pinnacled on the crest of noon
Crown'd with celestial flame   .   .   .
                                        *Asklepios!*

To-day the discrown'd gold of my hair is strewn
In the green lap of grasses, my bowed brow
Leans on the good strong shoulder of the earth
Even as a stricken mortal's might, that seeks
His comfortable mother in his grief.
Earth, earth, what flower from seed wilt thou put forth
Fed by the waters of mine eyes, that most
Shoot lightnings? dews wrung from the Sun-god's eyes,
Divinely wrathful, mortally unhappy!

*Asklepios! my son! Asklepios!*

I am a God.   Admetos is a King.
The God came to the King's doors overnight
And knocked and was admitted ; and the King
Knew me and asked my will.
                          " To be thy servant
Throughout a year of days," I answered him.

72

" Phœbus-Apollo, how shall this thing be? "
I said : " I slew a smith, a monstrous clod,
Not God or mortal, one that had done evil.
I am the avenger of evil among the Gods,
For this one and for that I have stretched my bow
And winged my arrow through the heart of Wrong;
But this was evil done unto myself,
And Vengeance wore the sleek face of Advantage,
Wherefor Zeus robs me of my Godhead, King,
And I will be thy shepherd for a year."
He stood half wonderstruck, half shamed-protesting,
But I bade him bring me out among his flocks
And speak no more.
              "I will have peace," I said.

"Fear not, and bid thy people not to fear;
For I am worn with too much strife and passion,
And no more hurt shall come from that I do.
Thou shalt not suffer by this term of service,
But see thy lands grow rich and bountiful,
And where thou lov'st I'll win thy love for thee,
And life shall prosper with thee,
                   " Life is sweet !
Make it not too sweet, God, lest when death come
It look more bitter than my soul can bear."
" Even death, Admetos, I'll delay for thee.
Now, peace ! I am done with vengeance for a space."
Thus I am come again upon the earth
Even as a common man   .   .   .

*Asklepios!*

The people eye me timidly, and dare
Not consort with the God they may not worship.
Even so it was in those first days of life
When I was a boy in Delos with my Mother,
And only half aware I was a God.
O this unconquerable loneliness
That binds the crown of Godhead on our brows!
Yet easier the aloofness of the people
Than the familiar face of the half-God Pan.
I met in the woods the brute-divinity,
Who fleered an impudent hoof, a satyr-smile
Licking his lips:

     " What, Helios! is the sun
Debased to something lower than the earth?
What! are we two, I of the beast's grain, thou
The delicate, disdainful spirit of flame,
The seed of mischief and the seed of Zeus,
Brought equal at the last? Nay, is the beast
Sun's master, Helios? Shepherds are my subjects.
I do not sway high kingdoms of the air—
I drag my hoofs in the clay. I do not fashion
Songs for the stars upon a golden lyre—
I (as did Marsyas, ha?) scrape out rough tunes
On common reeds. I am not beautiful,
I have not eyes like June-blue heavens on fire,
Nor hair filched from the harvest of the sun,
Nor a white matchless shape, supple and swift

74

And strong and splendid.  I am an earthy thing,
Half goat and half coarse boor, not fit to touch
The sun's moon-sister—(yet, who knows? who knows!
Let her keep watch on Latmos how she will
Above the slumbers of her pretty shepherd !)
No, Pan is not as Helios!  Helios is
A shepherd, sister'd by a shepherd's wanton,
And Pan's a King, and shepherds are his subjects ! "

Zeus, did it feed thy pride on proud Olympos,
Did it pleasure thee to hear the brutish God,
The disgustful animal we chafe to name
A God even as ourselves, thus flout thy son ?

*Asklepios ! dead son ! Asklepios !*
Doomed to the solitariness of greatness
We watch, we lonely Gods on shrouded heights,
The careful, padded steps, the little lives,
The little trivial lives of men and women
That fear our anger and entreat our favour;
And while we are indifferent all is well,
And if we rise to hate all is not ill,
But when we stoop to meet uplifted eyes
Of bright aspiring fools that will not choose
To tread life's inconspicuous middle ways—
O, when we love we bring our lov'd ones woe

I had a son, his name was Phaeton.
Could he be of my being and not be proud ?
He was all inspiration, and he mounted

Up to the highest and reached his hands for the sun
And shouted : "I will light the fires in heaven!"
But he was three-parts man to one-part God,
So men and Gods shrugged his brief blaze of glory
Into extinction . . . Thus I lost my son,
Phaeton, killed thro' overmuch ambition.

I had a son, his name was Orpheus.
Could he be of my being and not love?
His love was rooted deeplier than Hell.
He said : "I will pluck back my love from Hell
Tho' it upheave all Hell in the plucking." When
He failed, being one-part man to three-parts God,
He chose the swift way to regain his love
And died a vile death . . . Thus I lost my son,
Orpheus, killed thro' too great love and longing.

I had a son. He was Asklepios,
Could he be of my being and not ᴋɴᴏw?
His wisdom girdled life and death in one ;
Life smiled on him, because he smiled on death
And said : "Life is less conquerable than death."
He said : "I will reverse the word of death."
He said : "I will make the dead to live again."
Two days ago Asklepios lived . . .
                                        The King
Of the nether-world, that wears the face of night
An    hates me, wearing day's face, called on Zeus :
" This mortal steals upon my sovereignty,

Stands brazen champion for the world of flesh,
Determines souls that waver towards the Styx—
Worse! hales the souls back from beyond the Styx,
Bringing the dead to life.   This is more craft,
Brother, than we may suffer in a man.
Shall he with careless finger sway at will
The Balance of Destiny?   Avenge me, Zeus!"
A Cyclops forged a thunder-bolt for Zeus,
And, black-browed, Zeus did launch it  .  .  .  Thus
My son Asklepios, killed thro' too much knowledge.

*Asklepios! my dead Asklepios!*

Let the dark King of Stygia howl for aid
To Olympos! I am King of Heaven and ask
No aid! I wreak my vengeance for myself.
I rose up in the wrath of my bereavement
And set an arrow to the silver bow
That none save I can bend, and let it fly.
I might not slay the wielder of the bolt,
But I did slay the forger of the bolt.
And when I saw the Cyclops pierced and dead
I came to Zeus and told him of my deed :
"Father, 'gainst whom my bow was never turned,
Father, that hast destroyed thine own son's son,
I defy thy doing and have destroyed thy tool."

Then while the Gods stood all aghast, Zeus spake :
"Go from among this immortal company

Which thou hast sinned against in daring so
To sin against *me* that am the head of all,
And learn to quell thy too fierce spirit, learn
To teach thy riotous blood obedience,
Serving the sons of men one year of days.
Go hence! thou art not of us for twelve moons."
I nothing said, and went.   For when we Gods
Revolt among ourselves the end is near,
And Zeus must levy justice as he will.

*Asklepios! my dead Asklepios!*
*Had an hundred bolts been forged instead of one*
*I had slain an hundred Cyclops for thy sake*
*And suffered an hundred years of degradation!*

Earth that receivest my body for a space,
I first saw light upon thee.   Comfort me,
And tame a little the untamed blood in me.
Better will I endure to learn of thee
Than of the envious Gods, whom this disgrace
Serves for a secret feast to glut their hearts on.
For we have loved each other, thou and I,
And I have belted thee with golden arms,
And I have claspt thee daily with hot kisses,
And felt thee leap and pulse and answer to me
Like a shy maid grown bold and glad with love.
There's that in the core of thee that is so kin
To the core of me, it holds us twain inseverable,
Tho' from a billion blue-gold caverns of air

## APOLLO IN PHERAE

Translucent waves of space roll up an ocean
'Twixt earth and sun: our hearts beat time together.
My sister of the spheres has no such power
To quicken thee, be lov'd of thee and love thee.
She rains down light like argent snows; and thou,
Part shadow'd, part-illumin'd, wholly chill'd,
Submitt'st thyself to call her queen, who asks
No ardent service of thee, earth, as I do.
Yet, chaste twin-sister, we were of one birth;
Thy veins run all the silver, mine the gold.
What marvel Leto had nine days labour of us,
Strenuously thus disparting snow from flame,
To give the Gods one daughter all pure ice,
One son all perfect fire?   .   .

                  O Thunderer!
That spark of immortal fire which, pregnant in her,
Evolved into my Godhead, issuèd
Out of *thy* Godhead; my humiliation
Is thy humiliation, Zeus! I stand
Supremest in thy shining progeny:
I am thy glittering symbol fix'd in heaven
To draw the dazed, adoring eyes of men:
I am thy arm of vengeance, I the hand
Bestowing thy good gifts: I am thy Voice
Of mystic prophecy and divination
Thro' which thou keep'st thy fingers on men's souls.
Daughters and sons thou hast whose attributes,
This one by twisty cunning, this by love

Too often base, this by remorseless carnage
Not bearing the high name of vengeance, these
By the insidious lusts of gold and wine,
Serve to express thee to the bodies of men;
But I express thee to the ghost in them,
For there is none whose vesture is like mine
Weft only of the spirit's highest tissues,
So that the world beholding thee thro' me
Beholds thee at thy zenith, and exalted
Out of the flesh struggles to sense an instant
The music, fire and essence of Olympos.
This Thunderer, wilt thou smirch? More dim, more dim
Than the imperial spark thou quenchest in me
Thou mak'st thy imperial fires whence I did spring,
The fount of us so indissoluble
That what shames thee shames me.

                                        Earth, is this vengeance?

Nay, I see clearer. Rest unstained of me,
Thou God that art the father of my being.
The spirit of me, which is *Thou*, makes cause with thee
Against me. We must be inviolable
Or men will point their fingers —when We fall.

*Asklepios! farewell, Asklepios!*

Earth, I will serve on thee my year of days
Nor chafe beneath them like a petulant boy.
Ay, tho' Zeus force my Godhead into bonds
I will yet bear my bondage like a God.